CHRISTOPHER **BERG**

ISBN 13: 978-1-931945-80-6
ISBN 10: 1-931945-80-2

Library of Congress Catalog Number: 2007941204

Printed in the United States of America

First Printing: December 2007

12 11 10 09 08   5 4 3 2 1

Andover,
Minnesota

Expert Publishing, Inc.
14314 Thrush Street NW,
Andover, MN 55304-3330
1-877-755-4966
www.expertpublishinginc.com

DEDICATIN

To my parents, Dave and Sue

To my wife, Beth

To my children, Emily and Kate

I love you all beyond words.

CNTENTS

Acknowledgments.................................... ix

Introduction xi

F **Family First**
—Prioritize Your Life, Strive for Balance........ 1

O **Only What Really Matters**
—Block out the Noise and Teach
the Important Lessons...............................23

C **Care More Than Anyone Else**
—Leading By Example 37

U **Undivided Attention**
—Be Present—Stay Connected 41

S **Say I Love you**
—Don't Underestimate the
Power of Your Words 57

Final Thoughts.....................................63

About the Author 67

ACKNWLEDGMENTS

One my core beliefs is that nothing worth accomplishing comes without the help of others. When I began this adventure I knew very little about writing a book or the publishing process. What I had was a strong belief I had been called to spread a message about the crucial role fathers play in their children's lives.

An amazing thing has happened along the way. Every time I had questions or doubts, I was introduced to the person who could help me through the particular stage I was at. Without the following people, *The FOCUSed Father* would not be a reality.

My parents, Dave and Sue, provided me an environment of unconditional love, and I thank them for being the ultimate role models for me and my siblings.

A special thank you to my wife, Beth, who is my partner in everything I do. I love you.

To Emily and Kate, thank you for making me the luckiest dad in the world. I love you.

To family and friends who read the first manuscript and provided honest, insightful feedback, thank you for pushing me to write a better book.

Thank you to the following individuals for sharing their fatherhood stories: Adam Carlson, Jay Fleischmann, Howard Quinlan, and Scott Weldy.

To the Focused Father men's group at Messiah United Methodist Church, especially Pastor Steve Richards, thank you for inspiring me through our many fatherhood discussions.

Thank you to my publishers, Harry and Sharron Stockhausen. Thank you for your guidance and expertise.

Special thanks to Greg Rye, Barbara Carlson, and Carol Bergenstal, who were the first non-family members to hear me say, "I want to write a book about fatherhood." Along the way, they provided valuable feedback and connected me with others who were instrumental in making *The FOCUSed Father* a reality.

INTRDUCTION

Fatherhood: The Greatest Journey

The simple message of this book is that fathers must be active and involved in their children's lives, through a clear FOCUS on them. If you are looking for a step-by-step book on how to be a perfect dad, you've got the wrong book. Actually there *is* no book that can do that, as there is no such thing as a perfect dad. All we can do is strive for excellence in our effort. I ask you to open your mind to the possibility that being an involved dad is not as elusive as you might think, nor does it require giving up other aspects of your life.

I believe if we put our **F**amily first, pay attention to **O**nly what really matters, **C**are more than anyone else, give our **U**ndivided attention, and **S**ay I love you often, we have a foundation for parenting our children to bright futures.

Something I believe in strongly is the joy of fatherhood cannot be truly understood until you actually become a father. If you're a dad reading this, I'm willing to bet you agree with that premise. Even when you learn you're going to be a dad for the first time, you can't fully comprehend what is ahead for you. No doubt friends, family members, co-workers (or people you meet on airplanes for that matter) will try to tell you how different your life will be once you become a parent. They say things like, "Enjoy them while they are young; they grow up fast." If you are like me, you nodded your head in agreement and smiled. But, you had no comprehension of what those words really meant. For a yet-to-be dad reading this, count on these types of interactions. But do something I didn't do, and look into the eyes of the person saying these things and soak in their excitement. They already know the sheer joy of fatherhood you will soon experience.

Regardless of whether or not you are a dad yet, my hope for you is that this book inspires you to greatness as a father. Greatness, not measured by how many toys you buy or how many expensive vacations you take, but rather greatness measured by how present and involved you are in your child's life, what values you instill, and the love and encouragement you show on a daily basis.

The reason I feel qualified to deliver this message is I am the product of FOCUSed fatherhood. Growing up, my dad was actively involved in my life on a daily basis. He taught me important values, both through his words and through his actions. He coached many of my baseball and football teams, and when he wasn't a coach, he attended nearly every (seriously, he might have only missed a couple in my entire childhood) baseball, football, and basketball game I played in. But above all, my father was simply there for me **all the time.** Much of the person I have become is due to my parent's FOCUSed approach to parenting. No, I haven't won the Nobel Peace Prize, cured cancer, or won the Pulitzer Prize (at least not yet), but I am one of the happiest, most optimistic people you will meet. Don't even talk to me about whether or not the glass is half full or half empty. In turn, I am imparting that attitude on my children, and know it will serve them well in the long run. I strongly feel our greatest responsibility as parents is to prepare our children for adulthood. I implore you to give your children the great advantage of a positive attitude that my parents instilled in me.

I hope you read this book with an open mind and heart and see this book as part of your fatherhood journey, rather than the answer to all your questions. While I readily admit not having all the answers on "how,"—nobody has all the answers—I have a firm grasp and deep conviction on "how come," when it comes to fatherhood. It doesn't take a genius to understand that children benefit immeasurably from an involved father, and my primary goal is to inspire you to seek deep, ongoing interaction with your children.

The Importance of This Book

Some say we have a fatherhood, or lack of fatherhood, epidemic in America. I don't know if this is true, but I intend on doing my part to infect fathers with the notion that they must be actively involved in their children's lives. As you read, please keep this one thought in mind: Above all else, just *being present* for your children is your greatest gift to them as a father.

The importance of a book about fatherhood can be found when examining various studies regarding father involvement in children's lives.

In an analysis of nearly one hundred studies on parent-child relationships, father love (measured by children's perceptions of paternal acceptance/rejection, affection/indifference) was as important as mother love in predicting the social, emotional, and cognitive development and functioning of children and young adults:

- Having a loving and nurturing father was as important for a child's happiness, well-being, and social and academic success as having a loving and nurturing mother.
- Withdrawal of love by either the father or the mother was equally influential in predicting a child's emotional instability, lack of self-esteem, depression, social withdrawal, and level of aggression.
- In some studies, father love was actually a better predictor than mother love for certain outcomes, including delinquency and conduct problems, substance abuse, and overall mental health and well-being.
- Other studies found that, after controlling for mother love, father love was the sole significant predictor for certain outcomes, such as psychological adjustment problems, conduct problems, and substance abuse.[1]

According to the National Fatherhood Initiative (www.fatherhood.org) , children with involved, loving fathers are significantly more likely to do well in school, have healthy self-esteem, exhibit empathy and pro-social behavior, and avoid high-risk behaviors such as drug use, truancy, and criminal activity compared to children who have uninvolved fathers.

Finally, consider these facts:

- 90% of runaway children come from fatherless homes
- 71% of high school dropouts come from fatherless homes
- 85% of youth in prison come from fatherless homes
- 90% of inmates on death row come from fatherless homes

Statistics like these make it impossible to overestimate the impact we fathers have on our children.

---

[1] Rohner, Ronald P., and Robert A. Veneziano. "The Importance of Father Love: History and Contemporary Evidence." *Review of General Psychology* 5.4 (December 2001): 382-405.

In October 2006, there was a week of significant school violence in America. Six young girls in Pennsylvania were murdered, and one sixteen-year-old girl was killed in Colorado. More recently, more than thirty people were killed on the Virginia Tech campus. These tragedies, like other school shootings, boggle the mind. While most of the media stories centered on making schools safer through better gun control and security, I had a different, overwhelming concern: How does one become a killer? What triggers these thoughts in their heads that they should go to schools and kill innocent people? What kind of relationships do these people who kill have with their parents? Did they feel connected? I am in no way trying to over-simplify what is likely a complex series of events leading these men to kill. While I am no doctor, it's probably safe to say they were clinically mentally ill. However, I feel strongly that if we fathers are connected to our children, and remain connected as they become adults, the chances of someone committing travesties like these will be diminished.

A few introductions at this point will be helpful. As of this writing, I have been married to the love of my life, Beth, for fifteen years. We were great friends prior to marriage and have become best friends in marriage. Our marriage is the foundation on which our family rests, and, without her, I would be a fraction of the father I am. We have two beautiful children, Emily and Kate (ages eleven and eight, respectively, at the time of publication). It is with their permission that I share stories about them illustrating the joys, challenges, and awesome responsibility of fatherhood.

As you read, do so with the understanding that my views and opinions come mostly from personal experiences. Obviously, based on the ages of my children, my fatherhood experiences only span a decade. However, keep in mind that I have been the benefactor of an involved, committed father thirty-nine plus years. While you can apply much of the FOCUSed fatherhood concept to older children, I make no claims that I know what the challenges are to raising teenagers. I plan on writing that book once I gain the practical experience.

In addition to building a world of FOCUSed fathers, I hope to raise a great deal of money for child-related charities. For every book sold, one dollar goes to The FOCUSed Father Foundation (FFF). I have a goal to raise $1 million through the sale of this book, the sale of related items (available on the FOCUSed Father website, www. focusedfather.com), fundraising events, and donations. Yes, that's a lot of money. But with a strong sense of purpose, and the help of others, I believe anything is possible. Please buy a copy as a gift for someone else, and then tell everyone you know about this book and the FOCUSed Father Movement.

FOCUS

Family First
Prioritize Your Life, Strive for Balance

Family First

In order to be a FOCUSed father, you must understand and acknowledge that your family comes first. Not work. Not golf, fishing, or hunting. Putting family first puts you in the right frame of mind when making decisions about how you spend your time each day, week, and month. This does not mean you don't place high value on work and your personal interests. These are important aspects to life, and help give you a healthy balance. However, as a father whose *FOCUS is on fatherhood*, it is your responsibility to teach life lessons, and lead by example, preparing your children for the life ahead of them. This requires a great deal of time, and that time is only made available by placing family number one when it comes to your priorities. I recently went through the simple exercise of posting my priorities in my office, just in case I needed reminding:

1. **Family and Faith**

2. **Work**

3. **Volunteer Activities**

4. **My Time**

We all need a compass to give us direction in life, and writing down your priorities will give you just that. Your complete list might differ from mine, but I encourage you to make sure your number one is the same as mine.

Did your father attend all of your football games, basketball games, concerts, or recitals? Or, was he rarely present at these types of events? Regardless of your personal experience, I'm sure you wished your father was in attendance all the time.

Before you call your dad and give him a hard time about the number of games he missed, understand that the generation before us (the great Baby Boomer generation) didn't always have the same choices we enjoy. Companies were not as family-centric as they are today. It was often the exception, not the rule, to leave thirty minutes early for the start of your child's evening activity. Whether a father traveled for work during the week, or spent his days in the office, rarely was the workweek altered to accommodate children's activities. I make no judgments about this. It's just the way it was.

Fortunately for our children, I believe the societal norm has changed for the better. Companies I have worked for over the last fifteen years have generally been very supportive and flexible with regard to my family-first attitude. Maybe I have just picked the right companies to work for or the right profession, but, in talking with many other men on this topic, I find they feel the same way. I take great pride in the fact that I have missed very few of my children's activities, but it hasn't just worked out this way by accident. Prior to planning business trips and my own activities, I check to see what is on the calendar for the kids and Beth. Simply put, I don't want to miss anything. I *choose* not to miss anything. While it is very fulfilling for me to watch my children participate in music and sports, I know the benefit to Emily and Kate of my presence is immeasurable.

Howard, a father of four, gives an excellent example of what it means to live your priorities:

I remember a few years ago when I was approached about an opportunity to become a board member for a well-known charitable organization. This position not only carried important responsibilities, it also required a fairly extensive time commitment. I began to weigh this opportunity carefully against my other commitments, not the least of which was the significant travel my job required. And since I was out of town so often, there were limited types of activities of this nature that I could consider. Nonetheless, I was very flattered by the offer as I was also intrigued by the networking opportunities this type of position would undoubtedly provide.

After speaking with my wife and a number of people about this position, I was ready to accept the offer when another, incredibly unique offer came to me literally out of left field. I was picking up my twelve-year-old daughter from an initial meeting of her new traveling fast pitch softball team, when she came running from the outfield to my car with a breathless request. Between her gasps for air she began her story of how good her team was, but how they desperately needed a coach. She had already concluded that her team, while admittedly not the greatest collection of players, was certainly good enough to play against some of the better teams and be competitive. Still, this group of players felt that they needed just the right person, and I was that person. In fact, she had already spoken with her team-mates about this situation, and had gotten their unanimous approval of me as the candidate they wanted to coach the team!

As I gave her the standard "I'll think about it" line, she pressed her case further. In doing so, I began to see that her request had a personal element that made me feel both proud that she thought so highly of me, and melancholy by the fact that she was growing up and would probably not need me as a coach in the near future. As we drove home, we recounted my coaching experiences with my daughter's older sibling, and how she wanted to replicate those experiences and how much fun we would have with this team. While this conversation continued, I began to think about the other opportunity that also required my response very quickly. As complimented as I was to have such wonderful choices, I knew I could never take on both responsibilities because each would require so much of my time. So there I was, caught between the horns of the proverbial dilemma. The charitable organization would provide many positive contributions and, on the other hand, in a much smaller venue, the coaching position would also provide some help for the girls.

To make matters worse, I knew I could probably placate my daughter by insisting that I was too busy, that my travel schedule was too unreliable, and that I had been considering a voluntary position with the charitable organization that she knew and would certainly endorse. So what was a father to do? The answer, as I always found, came from a quick analysis of what my heart told me to do: Family comes first and, in the end, is the guiding principle.

When you think about it, all dads are kind of coaches within the framework of the family. My children look to me for guidance, instruction, rules, discipline, and preparation—just as they do from a coach in an activity or sport. As dads, we share victories and losses with our children, and we try to impart wisdom in the wake of these outcomes. And, of course, we stress the importance of teamwork within the family dynamic.

So after this internal analysis, I told my daughter that I would accept her offer to coach their team. In doing so I was somewhat surprised that I had no regrets about turning down my other opportunity. In fact, I felt a profound sense of love and fulfillment that the other opportunity could never have matched when my daughter jumped into my arms with a shriek of elation saying, Oh, thank you, Dad. I love you so, so much!

The season was successful, and both the coach and the girls enjoyed themselves immensely. And because we all had so much fun, I continued my coaching experiences in other activities as well. Softball, baseball, golf, and hockey became part of our lives. And while I passed up other volunteer opportunities that certainly carried a higher profile, no other type of commitment could really match the fulfillment that I got each time my daughter or son told a friend he's my dad, but he also coaches my team. Or when I met a boy or girl who played on one of our teams and they greeted me warmly with a big smile and Hi, Coach!

Nothing compares to sitting on a dugout bench with your child, chewing sunflower seeds, and talking about whatever comes to mind. Indeed, the simplest things in life are the best!

So, what are your priorities?

My Priorities

_____

_____

_____

_____

_____

_____

_____

_____

_____

_____

_____

_____

_____

_____

_____

_____

_____

Marriage is the Foundation

One of the greatest gifts you can give your children is a positive, loving relationship that is based on mutual respect and ongoing communication with your wife. The foundation of your family is built on that relationship. This is vital to achieving balance, a topic I will cover later.

The primary way children learn about relationships is through observing the adults in their house. How do you communicate with your wife? If you are negative, condescending, or continually argumentative, your children learn that as appropriate behavior. Rather, if you show great love and caring as you interact, your children will learn that too.

Unfortunately, not everyone stays married. My parents divorced when I was in my late twenties. However, while I was growing up, my parents set an excellent example for me and my siblings (I am the oldest of three). I do not remember them fighting, raising a voice, or demeaning each other in our presence. Of course they must have had disagreements, as all couples do, but they dealt with them in private. What I observed was a relationship consisting of love and mutual respect, and I am certain this greatly influenced who I am as a husband and father.

Setting positive examples is one of the overriding themes of this book, and positive spousal interaction and communication is vital to our children's development.

Be a Great Wife

Beth and I have an ongoing inside joke, poking fun at traditional gender roles.

When we began having children both of us worked full time. As a cardiac nurse in a hospital, Beth often worked evenings, weekends, and night shifts. As a result of this, I was very active in our children's lives from the start. Other than breast feeding, we shared most other baby responsibilities equally—diapers, baths, bottle feeding, rocking, etc. While I didn't necessarily realize it then, the time I had alone with Emily and Kate early on allowed me to fulfill some of the roles traditionally performed by women. Although I didn't choose this (it was more a result of Beth's work schedule), I feel blessed for this to have taken place. You, on the other hand, can *choose* to share the baby-related duties, as well as other household duties that might be normally associated with women and moms. Not only will your children benefit now and in the future, but your marriage will also benefit.

Back to the joke: Whenever Beth sees me folding laundry, making dinner, or cleaning, she says "Have I told you lately you're a great wife?"

The Power of Focus

I am currently employed in a sales role with a major financial services company. My job is to create partnerships with investment representatives. When they sell my products to individual investors, I am doing my job well.

2005 was a record year for me, as I nearly doubled sales in my territory from the year before. While I attribute this rapid growth to a few things, there is one factor that I point to above all else: Focus. Prior to August of 2004, I had sales responsibilities for multiple product lines. I was experiencing a little success in each product line, but not the great success I was striving for.

In the summer of 2004, I was told I would be marketing just one product. While I was skeptical of giving up the other products, it turned out to be the best thing that happened to me. I gained a laser-like focus on my new role. I knew exactly what the recipe for success was, and my clients knew exactly what I expected of them. That was the driving force behind my record growth the following year.

In order to be great fathers, we must have that laser-like focus on our children. This does not mean we give our children everything they want, or give up all non-child related activities in our life. But it means we factor in the question "How does this affect my child?" when making decisions about where or how we spend our time.

Find Passion

Hopefully you are as passionate about your family as I am about mine. I encourage you to find other passions as well.

Maybe it's your job, maybe it's a hobby, or maybe it's an athletic endeavor. Whatever it is, find something **for you**, while keeping your passion for family foremost.

Perhaps you remember the story about a former NFL player. His dad trained him to be a professional football quarterback from a very early age. From everything I have read his father was consumed with seeing his son grow up to be in the NFL. This child was not allowed to watch cartoons and never touched a Big Mac. Do you think his dad had other passions beyond making his son an NFL quarterback? Do you think his father's obsession was healthy for the child? Can you imagine the pressure of living your life for the fulfillment of a parent? I'm sure some readers do know that pressure.

Yes, as you may already know, he became a pro quarterback. But after only a few years in the NFL he had problems with drugs, was out of the league, and has had multiple stints in jail.

Bottom Line: Be your child's biggest fan and supporter, and help them find their passion. However, don't try to live your life through them. *Find your own passion!*

Balance

Playing basketball and golf (my passions) most of my life, I know the importance of having good balance. In order to consistently make jump shots, or effectively hit a golf ball, my legs need to be a certain width apart, creating a solid foundation, keeping me balanced. This same concept can be applied to fatherhood.

In my life I strive to be many things. Most importantly I aim to be a good husband, father, and employee. In order to do that, I need to give each of these areas significant attention. Additionally, I have a strong belief in the need to take care of myself physically and mentally (the "my time" priority I mentioned earlier). When I am able to successfully direct my time and energy in correct proportion, as dictated by my priorities list, to each of these areas, I feel my life is in good order. However, overloading any one of these causes me to be out of balance, and leads to stress and conflict in our house.

Just as a wheel needs to be round to roll evenly and consistently, our lives need the same balance for optimal performance. If I work excessively, I might lack the time to be an involved father or committed husband. If I don't work enough, I jeopardize success in my business, which could ultimately affect my ability to support our family from a financial standpoint. Too much time on my interests, and I am neither a good husband and father nor a good employee. Being excessive about *my* interests is without a doubt the worst area to overload, and creates the worst imbalance.

One excellent idea for keeping balance in your life comes from Adam, a father of two young children, who has found a way to turn "my time" into "our time."

I have two young children, Brendan, who is three, and Svea, who is one. I grew up with horses, have horses, and love to live the country life-style. When our first child was born, I thought to myself, I can either ride by myself, not be with my son or wife, and have my wife mad at me, or I could take them with me. Brendan started riding at five weeks and LOVES to go horseback riding! Svea started at seven weeks, and she really loves to go too. Sometimes I'll be riding on the trail with Svea in the child backpack and Brendan is riding in front of me. I think, if I can get my kids interested in the things I want to do during "my time," then, hopefully, they'll want to do that when they get older. This helps create another family activity and helps dad continue doing what he loves and maybe I can get our kids passionate about that too. I have some friends who have given up their hobbies because of their kids, and I don't think that is necessary. Here's my disclaimer about taking kids horseback riding as infants. I only did that because I feel very comfortable on our horses. We have had the two horses that we take our kids on for ten plus years and know how they are going to react. Obviously I wouldn't put my children's safety in jeopardy.

At times, balance can be very difficult to achieve. Life does not always roll along smoothly, and, inevitably we all experience times where we are out of balance. The first step to regaining balance is to acknowledge that you are out of balance. Next, pull out your priority list to get your compass pointing in the right direction again. At the risk of stating the obvious, make sure your number one priority gets the most attention. If you are following the premise of the book to this point, that priority should be family. Try keeping a weekly log, tracking how your time is spent each day. You might be surprised what it reveals. Next, incorporate the input of others. Ask your wife how she sees your time being spent. Ask those same questions of other important people in your life whose opinions you value. Sometimes we forget that life's challenges are not unique to us. Someone else you know has felt imbalanced at times.

Run Your Life—Don't Let Your Life Run You

Balance, as I have discussed, is not always easy to achieve, nor does it happen by accident. Choose carefully what activities you become involved in. Saying yes to everything, no matter how great the cause, will, no doubt, pull you away from important family time. Don't misunderstand me, I think it's important to be involved in the community, church, and other charitable causes. Just don't make your involvement at the sacrifice of your children.

I know people who have agreed to participate on every committee and help plan every event because it felt like the right thing to do. They are people with noble intentions. They are also people who oftentimes run from their jobs to meetings, and from meetings to their jobs. Where does fatherhood fit in? Unfortunately, for these people fatherhood becomes primarily a weekend activity.

Don't let the tail wag the dog! Carefully select the number of things you volunteer to do, and take time to understand how they impact your time at home.

Selfishness and Busyness

We are blessed (pun intended) to belong to a wonderful church, with a wonderful lead pastor, Steve Richards. Steve came to our church, Messiah United Methodist (Plymouth, Minnesota) in 2000, and brought with him a sense of urgency. This urgency was not to accomplish one specific thing, but rather to make our congregation much more than it was in all facets. At the top of Steve's list was to provide a children's ministry second to none. Everything from Sunday school, to choir, to vacation bible school is better today than it was prior to Steve's arrival. His philosophy, and rightly so in this author's opinion, is that the best time to have a meaningful impact in a person's life is when the person is a child. All of Messiah's children have benefited from the leadership Steve has provided.

In addition to his impact on children, Steve also gives some of the best Sunday morning sermons one will ever hear. Some pastors give great sermons that quote scripture and tell stories from the Bible. However, Steve gives great sermons using stories from the Bible that illustrate an important message for our lives, giving us practical ideas for the coming week.

In one of his sermons he used the phrase "selfishness and busyness," two topics that most definitely impact fatherhood. With Steve's permission, here is a portion of that sermon:

Two of the barriers to forming and sustaining relationships are self-ishness and busyness. Selfishness exists whenever I expect the world to revolve around me. And busyness is really another way of seeing that life is all about me. Busyness shrinks my vision of others by shrinking my willingness to expend energy for someone else.

Remember the images of the clock and the compass: The clock is our commitments, schedules, and activities, and the compass is our values and priorities. How many of us have a personal compass that values others, but then we allow the clock to rule our lives? So we conserve our energy for our needs, and we make excuses for not getting involved in someone else's life. One day, Jesus told a story about some very righteous, faith-filled individuals who had no time to stop to help someone whose life was in danger—and in the process of following the clock, living lives focused on me, they lost their lives. Yes, we have limits. We can't save everyone. We can't be everyone's friend, but we've got a problem whenever we use our own busyness as an excuse for not getting involved.

Being a FOCUSed father requires you put your children's needs ahead of yours much of the time. For some, this is a huge adjustment. Trust me, it is one worth making. Don't become the father who is just too busy with work to give his children his full attention and energy. That selfishness will take you down a path leading nowhere.

Family Mission Statement

Through parenting classes Beth and I have taken, and books we have read, it became clear to us that a family mission statement was imperative for our family.

A family mission statement is similar to a company mission statement, which you are probably familiar with. It defines what is most important about being part of your family. In other words, it describes what you stand for. For our family it reminds us, and tells others, what our family values are. How we conduct ourselves, and make decisions as a family, are driven by the statement. It serves as the compass Steve referred to in his sermon.

I share our family mission statement with you as an example. We chose to use the letters of our last name, as well as included Bible verses to support the four key areas. This is only one way to form a statement. If your children are old enough to have input, be sure to include them as you write your family mission statement.

Berg Family Mission Statement:

Be kind to everyone

So now I am giving you a new commandment: Love each other. Just as I have loved you, you should love each other. Your love for one another will provide to the world that you are my disciples. John 13:34 (NLT)

Education—School, church, music

It takes wisdom to have a good family, and it takes understanding to make it strong. It takes knowledge to fill a home with rare and beautiful treasures. Proverbs 24:3-4 (NCV)

Respect yourself and others

Teach [your children] to exercise self-control, to be worthy of respect, and to live wisely. They must have a strong faith and be filled with love and patience...And you yourself must be an example to them. Titus 2:2, 7 (NLT)

Give of your time, talents, and money

The righteous walk in integrity—happy are the children who follow them! Proverbs 20:7 (NLT)

Jay, the father of two young girls, shares the following story about how his family developed their mission statement:

My boss sent me on a business trip that required me to drive approximately four hours both ways. He recommended I listen to The Seven Habits of Highly Effective People *during the ride. I reluctantly agreed. He was the boss. Normally I would pass such time listening to music at high volume levels. Also, unfortunately for me, I may be quizzed on the material upon my return. Not listening was not an option.*

Around one hour into the trip, the subject of mission statements was presented. I was half-listening, unenthused with useless corporate mission statements when I began wondering, why don't we have family mission statements? I mean, is there a more vital organization than the family? Enthused by my realization, I immediately pulled over to the side of the interstate and began drafting our first family mission statement. The timing could not have been more appropriate as our first daughter was only months old. One hour later, I had finished and I was more jazzed up than ever. That evening when I returned home, I presented this mission statement to my wife, Amy, and excitedly advised her that this was how we were going to run our family. While it was a great mission statement, there was one problem: Amy had nothing to do with writing it. Nonetheless, that mission statement was framed and posted in the kitchen along with every occupied bedroom. Three and a half years went by when I realized that our mission statement was not implemented as effectively as it should have been. We now had Kaylee, our almost four-year-old and Avery, who was approaching two years old. We decided we needed a new mission statement that was developed by all four of us.

Over the next three months, we dedicated our family meetings to developing this new mission. All four of us, even our youngest, came up with single words that meant a lot to us such as, responsibility, proactive, and God. We ended up with a list of around thirty words. After a few more family meetings, we dwindled the list to the nine words that we felt should be the foundation from which we built our family. From these nine words, we developed our new mission statement. That was the day all four of us, not just me, became accountable to our mission statement. Again, Avery was not even two when it was written. Her input was minimal as she had not had an opportunity to really develop what she valued. As a result, we will continue to review and modify our mission statement, as a group.

Here is Jay's family's mission statement:

God—We will continue to learn about and give glory to Jesus.

Proactive—We will solve problems before they occur and not fall victim to circumstance.

Diversity—We will learn about people that are different from us.

Responsible—We are able to choose our own response.

Honesty—We will tell the truth.

Respect—We will be considerate of others and their things.

Tolerance—We will accept things for what they are and learn from them.

Communicate—We will listen first, share our ideas, then speak our opinion.

Accountable—We will take ownership for our actions and words.

Use the space provided here to get started on your family mission statement. Make sure you post it somewhere (or several places) in your house as a constant reminder to all.

Our Family Mission Statement

_____

_____

_____

_____

_____

_____

_____

_____

_____

_____

_____

_____

_____

_____

_____

Faith and Fatherhood

My faith is the engine that drives my value system. While it is possible to be a great father without a strong faith, there may be something missing. While I am Christian, I make no judgments about your particular religion. That you believe there is a Higher Power at work acknowledges, for me, that which is hard to deny: There is too much beauty in this world for it all to be accidental.

Regardless where you are in your own personal faith journey, please expose your children to religion. If you didn't grow up going to church, or if you haven't attended for a while, I encourage you to attend worship at a few churches in your area. Meet the pastors, and meet some of members.

Emily and Kate are benefiting immeasurably from their experiences at church, and I know it is helping shape who they are and who they will become. In addition to learning about God, they are interacting with other adult role models that reinforce the values we are teaching at home.

In his book, *Parenting on Point*, James Williams describes the concept of a North Star. Each family's North Star serves as the moral center of family values, and helps guide them in all they do. While this goes hand-in-hand with the family mission statement concept, a North Star is almost by definition derived through faith-based concepts. James writes: "There's no question that less time together—and, consequently, a decrease in meaningful conversation between parents and children—is a major reason why things are more difficult for parents today. We all know that it takes time to love, nurture, and guide our children. Having a North Star helps us to be intentional about giving our children and our families the time and attention they need and deserve. It keeps us focused on the course we must follow if we are to stay on point and lead our families along the right path, the path God wants us to travel."

You Are Not Your Father

We have no choice about who our parents are. For some that's a blessing, and for others it's a challenge. Much about the people we are, and the parents we become, have to do with our parents' influence.

My hope is that your dad, like mine, has been a positive force in your life. If your dad has not been present in your life for whatever reason, it *does not* mean that you are, or will be, any less of a father to your children. The take-away here is that while some of us are given a great head start in becoming FOCUSed fathers because of our dad's approach to parenting, we all have the same opportunity to *choose* to be FOCUSed fathers.

Scott writes about his experience, which was different from mine:

We learn a lot, maybe all, about parenting from our parents. We males especially learn a lot from our fathers. This doesn't mean you have to have the same parenting style. My father was always very busy running the family farm. He was somewhat stoic and seemed to expect his kids would know what's expected of them, not a lot of heart-to-heart talks. But I've always used that experience to know how I didn't want to interact with my children. I want to always be around them and let them know I love them. A funny thing has happened; I believe that by my father seeing how I treat my kids he has learned that it's okay for a father to be loving and affectionate, not just the provider.

Take a minute to reflect upon the positive things your father did for you. Go ahead and write them down if you want. Now do the same thing for the less-than-positive things you recall. At the risk of being obvious, *do not* subject your children to the items on the negative side of that equation. For instance, as I previously mentioned, my father was in attendance at nearly all my games. We played catch in the backyard and shot hoops in the driveway. His presence and involvement was vital to my development in, and enjoyment of, those sports. On the flip side, my father wasn't always the most patient person. While I don't feel it hindered my development in any way, it was about the only thing I could come up with on the negative side—as I told you earlier, I have a great dad!

Unless I am out of town due to circumstances beyond my control, which is rare, I am present at Emily's and Kate's games and concerts, just as my dad was present at mine. Later in the book I will illustrate that having patience is not always easy for me, but something I work at.

Goals

Over the years I have read several motivational books. While none of them are exactly the same, one common theme is goal setting.

In order to actively pursue the life you want, you *must* have goals. These goals must be specific, measurable, achievable, and, most importantly, written. If you haven't written your goals down, what you really have are hopes. For example, I have a goal to shoot par for eighteen holes of golf. It fits the criteria because it's specific, measurable, achievable (my best score is one over par, so I only have to get one stroke better), and it's written (I have ten goals each year, written and posted on my bathroom mirror). If my goal was, "I want to be a better golfer," would that fit the criteria above? I don't think so. Even if it's written, and achievable, it is not measurable or specific. How would I *really* know if I were a better golfer?

Once you've written down your specific, measurable, achievable goals, there is one more step. Each of your goals needs an action plan. For instance, I have created a practice plan to achieve my goal of shooting par. It includes playing at least one round of golf each week during the Minnesota golf season, putting and chipping practice for thirty minutes once a week, and hitting balls at the practice range twice a week for thirty minutes each time. Emily and Kate are learning the game and Beth loves the game as I do, so we'll be practicing as a family. None of this guarantees I will reach my goal, but having a plan provides me the best chance.

How does all this goal setting relate to fatherhood? Goal setting goes hand-in-hand with priorities. Your priorities are a reflection of your core values, and your goals are priorities in action. Make sure that some of the goals you set are family-related. One of my goals each year is to volunteer in Emily and Kate's classrooms.

Get a pen out right now and starting writing down things you would like to see happen. Divide the list into short range (one year or under), and long range goals (anything greater than one year). Seriously, do it now in the space I have provided for you.

Short Range Goals

_____

_____

_____

_____

_____

_____

_____

_____

_____

_____

_____

_____

Long Range Goals

_____

_____

_____

_____

_____

_____

_____

_____

_____

_____

_____

Ask For Help–*All Great Accomplishments Involve The Help of Others*

While fatherhood is my greatest joy in life, I will concede that it is not always easy. There are challenges at all ages, and answers are not always apparent.

In early 2005, I embarked on a journey to complete a Sprint Distance Triathlon (on the goal list I mentioned earlier). In case you are not familiar, a triathlon consists of three different sports—swimming, cycling, and running. As I learned about triathlon, and those who competed in the sport, I discovered most competitors are already proficient in one of the three areas. I, on the other hand, was not accomplished in any of them, and quickly surmised that this would be my most difficult goal of the year. I renewed my membership to the local health club, and began swimming, cycling, and running.

From January 1 to June 12 (race day), I followed a training routine. At 8:15 a.m. I ran into the water with the forty-seven other competitors in my age group (to join and be joined by about five hundred other men and women). While others had described for me what it would be like to swim in a cool, dark lake with other competitors swimming on top of you, the reality of it caused me to panic. I found my way over to the nearest life guard (fortunately, there were many of them along the swim route), and uttered something like "I have to quit." At that moment I had decided there was no possible way I could complete the half-mile swim, given the fact that I wasn't even half way to the half way point. The life guard, the first of many I would meet that day, calmly said, "You can do this." I firmly believe it was those four words that made all the difference for me, jolting me into a better frame of mind. I had trained too hard to give up. I had sixteen family members and friends waiting for me back on shore, and I wasn't going to show up in the lifeboat! I created a new strategy, which was to simply get from one life guard to the next, which is a good life lesson for everyone. Don't try to take big steps all the time, just get from life guard to life guard.

I pulled myself out of the water thirty-six minutes from the time I went in, which was about fourteen minutes longer than I told Beth and kids it would take me. The bike and run portion were uneventful, and I crossed the finish line having accomplished my toughest goal of 2005. As I mentioned earlier, there were forty-eight competitors in my age group. Where did I finish in relation to the others, you might be wondering? Let's just say that shortly after that day, I had to change one of my computer passwords: cberg46.

As I reflected upon the triathlon journey, I realized how much help I had along the way. Some of it came without asking, but most came through my requests of others. Beth, as she always is, was the ultimate supporter. She was understanding as I went to the gym or went on a run. She was understanding as I ate healthy foods and passed on some of her awesome cooking. Then, there were the other triathletes I met during training. They helped me with my training plan, prepared me for race day, and gave me countless pieces of advice. Finally, there were the volunteers at the race, especially the life guards. Without help from all these people, and others, I don't think I could have completed the race.

In fatherhood we will be faced with challenges for which the answers might not be apparent. At these times, we must remember that it is okay to ask for help. For some reason we men tend to think that asking for help is a sign of weakness. The reality is that asking for help is a sign of *strength*. No great accomplishment (and eighteen plus years of raising a child is definitely an accomplishment) occurs without the help of others. Michael Jordan didn't win six NBA championships by himself. Bill Gates didn't build Microsoft by himself. Believe it or not, Tiger Woods is not winning all these golf tournaments by himself. He'd be the first to tell you he owes a great deal to parents, coaches, and teachers.

Ask other dads what they might do in your situation. Ask your dad what he'd do. Remember, there are plenty of guys you know who have already parented kids the age of yours.

Ask for help. Remember, some days the shoe will be on the other foot, and you will be asked to help someone else.

Please visit www.focusedfather.com to find additional resources for helping you deal with some of the tougher parenting issues.

Purpose

A few years ago I participated in a study group through our church that discussed Pastor Rick Warren's book, *The Purpose Driven Life*. I am sure you have read the book, or are at least aware of it. The basic premise is that each of us is on earth for a purpose. You are not an accident.

After a great deal of reflecting and pondering as to what *my* purpose is, I concluded that it is to share my passion for fatherhood, with the hope that I can positively affect countless fathers, families, and children. If this book, and other FOCUSed Father programs, gives other dads inspiration to be present and connected in their children's lives, the results could be mega-powerful.

If you are still searching for *your* purpose, perhaps it's just a matter of FOCUSing in on what's most important to you.

Chapter Review:
- Family always comes first.
- Being a present and connected father doesn't happen by accident.
- Take control of your life, and make choices that allow you to be a FOCUSed father.
- Create a life for yourself that allows you to be present and connected in your child's life.

FOCUS

Only What Really Matters
Block Out the Noise
and Teach the Important Lessons

The Noise

We live in a world today with many things competing for our children's attention. Television, the Internet, video games, magazines, and friends are examples of things that potentially create noise.

Noise is what causes interference with our compasses, sending us the wrong direction. Noise can be inconsistent with the values we are teaching. Noise can lead to our children following a star other than the North Star.

Television, as I discuss later, is not always the enemy. However, there are certain aspects and programming that can influence our children in ways that are not good. One simple piece of advice is know what your children are watching, and don't allow them to view programs (and channels) that project images and ideas inconsistent with your family's values.

The Internet is a great way for children to learn about the world. The amount of information available is endless. However, like television, certain websites are not appropriate for children. Be vigilant about what content you allow them to see, and set limits on computer time.

Much of the problem with magazines lies with the advertising. The companies purchasing advertising are projecting images they feel will sell their products. These images are often of scantily clad young, very thin people. It is easy for children to interpret these images as something they should strive for. Make sure your children are reading and viewing age-appropriate magazines. Teach them that everyone's body is different and develops at a different rate. Tell them that beauty is not about being thin, or wearing a lot of makeup—exterior qualities. Beauty is about being kind, generous, and focused on helping others, which are interior qualities.

I hope your children have many friends. I also hope your children have friends being raised with similar values as yours. However, inevitably your children will meet and play with kids from families unlike yours. Don't discourage this, as diversity should be welcomed, but understand that your children might be exposed to behaviors, attitudes, and language that are not consistent with what you are teaching. Don't allow your children to adopt these behaviors. Explain to them that every family is different, and in your family you follow the Family Mission Statement you and your family created together.

The bottom line: Help your children deal with the noise through keeping them focused on the family values you are instilling through on-going conversations and activities.

Television: Not the Enemy

There is nothing wrong with children watching television. Some might disagree with that statement. However, this section comes with some important qualifiers. Excessive television watching, just like excessive Internet surfing and video game playing, is a problem, as are age-inappropriate shows. And, on average, American children watch a lot of television. According to a 2005 Kaiser Family Foundation study, children ages eight to eighteen spend more time (forty-four and a half hours per week) in front of computer, television, and game screens than any other activity in their lives except sleeping. How much TV do you allow? Depends. Each family's situation is different. I'd encourage you to operate under the rule that if it *feels* like there's too much TV in your house, there probably is (assuming you are taking an honest look at the situation). The National Institute on Media and the Family provides some ideas for dealing with television:

- To prevent impulse watching, use the TV guide before turning on the set.
- Record TV shows for your child, so they have a backup when there is nothing appropriate on the television for them to watch.
- Keep television sets out of children's bedrooms.
- Two hours of quality television programming per day is the maximum recommended by the American Academy of Pediatrics.

Just as we should know who our kids are playing with, we need to know what they are watching. If your pre-teen children are watching anything on the Disney Channel, you are in good shape. If they are watching *The Simpsons*, grab the remote. One obvious way to know what shows are appropriate and consistent with the values you are teaching is to watch a little TV with children. Not only might you learn something yourself, but it's another way to spend time with your kids.

Perhaps you know families who don't allow their children to watch television at all. Maybe it works well for them. However, denying children exposure to something so prevalent in our society might be doing them more harm than good. Remember, we are preparing our children for the rest of their lives. Give them the best chance at understanding the world around them by exposing them to that world in as many ways as possible. Television, when used appropriately, can be a great learning tool.

Please visit the National Institute on the Media and Family at www. mediafamily.org for important information on how the media affects our children and ideas and strategies your family can implement to deal with the noise.

Values

Whether we like it or not, the older our children get, the more time they spend away from us. Day care, preschool, kindergarten, grade school, junior high, high school, college...somebody please slow down time. I implore you and your spouse to be the ones to instill values in your children, through teaching and leading. No matter how much you like their teachers, coaches, and friends, don't let them be the ones teaching your kids the core values that will shape them for a lifetime. That is *our* responsibility, as FOCUSed fathers, along with FOCUSed mothers.

Use the family mission statement as a starting point for defining what values are important to your family. Then, use everyday life events as teaching opportunities. Nearly every day something happens that involves values. Take the time to talk to your kids about the significance of these events.

Pray that you are fortunate to have others, like teachers, to reinforce what you teach, but don't rely on others to do your job.

Sacrifice

In the fall of 2005 we received word that Beth's eighty-eight-year-old grandmother was in poor health. After a day of discussions, we decided to take the kids out of school Thursday and Friday and make the twelve-hour drive from Minneapolis to Toledo, Ohio.

It would have been easier for Beth to jump on an airplane and go by herself. But, our children have developed relationships with their great grandparents, and we felt it was important for them to see "Grandma Pooh" before her condition worsened. Emily was not happy about being pulled out of school. There were several important school events, plus a birthday party on the weekend she would miss. We told her we were very sorry, but Grandma needed us in Ohio. This proved to be a classic teaching moment. There are many times in life when we need to put others' needs ahead of our wants. In a word, it's called sacrifice. It took a while for the message to sink in, but by the time we loaded up the car, Emily was on board with the plan.

Beth and I couldn't have been more proud of Emily when she gave Grandma Pooh, hooked up to IV's and in very poor health, a big hug and told her how glad she was to see her.

Don't let events like this go by without explaining to your children what sacrifice means. Learning to put others' needs before your wants is a critical life lesson, and one that will touch many aspects of their lives.

Justice

"No Fair!" As children we said it to our parents, and, if your kids are old enough, they have said it to you. I think we are all born with this "justice gene." We innately believe all things must be equal and the same, when compared to our siblings and friends. For example, if your sister got to stay up late on a given night, and you didn't, I'm sure you felt wronged and said to your parents, "That's not fair!" What is the standard response to "Not fair?" Life's not fair. While true, I'd suggest another approach. Rather than that quick response, take time to teach about fairness. The reality, and our children need to know this, is that throughout life all people are not treated the same. Sometimes it makes sense, and sometimes it doesn't. Regardless, the earlier our children understand this dynamic, the better they will be prepared to handle it.

And, in case you need it, I'm giving you permission to treat each of your children different from the other. They are each unique, special gifts, and should be treated as such.

Character

In September 2005, Hurricane Katrina pummeled the Gulf Coast, destroying historic cities like Biloxi and Gulfport, Mississippi. Many areas of New Orleans, Louisiana, were flooded and thousands of people who did not evacuate the city prior to the storm experienced a living hell. Many died. There were stories of looting, fighting, and even people killing each other as the condition of their surroundings (lack of food, water, and medical supplies) deteriorated by the hour. It is times like this when true character is revealed. Unfortunately, there are people who will reveal the worst of what we have in this great nation. They will steal, and become violent, taking advantage of the chaos that exists. However, I firmly believe that the overwhelming majority of people rise above dire circumstances to help others and reveal strong moral character.

Hopefully, you don't encounter life events as desperate as the Katrina aftermath. But, on a lesser scale we are often faced with opportunities to reveal our true character to our children. Some people use the term role model. While we verbally impact and shape our children, our actions are even more important. Did you tell the cashier at the supermarket that she gave you too much change? Did you leave a note on the windshield of the car you bumped in the parking lot? These are minor events, with major impact. How we fathers respond to these situations reveals our true character to our children.

Between words and actions, choose action. Our children are watching us.

Prejudice and Discrimination

Perhaps one of the most frustrating social issues for me is that we are still dealing with racism in the country. Without exception, teach your children that no one is to be judged by the color of skin or ethnic background. It is simply not acceptable. You cannot stay silent on this issue.

Do you know anyone today who prejudges people or is overtly racist? Who do you think they learned that from? We both know this often comes directly from observing a parent's behavior and attitudes. If your parents held prejudices you observed, *break the cycle*. Teach your children we are all created equal and are all equally important. Teach your children that none of us has any choice in what color or nationality we are.

While this is the greatest nation on planet earth, not everyone is treated the same in twenty-first century. The Civil Rights Movement helped move us in the right direction, but there are still many miles to be traveled on the road to true equality. My hope and prayer is that our children's generation is the greatest yet when it comes to this issue. It is incumbent upon us to help get them started on that road.

Education

The value of education is one of the most important we can instill in our children. Their future depends on it. Education comes from daily interactions and experiences, as well as in the classroom. Both are important to the growth of your children.

Life Experiences Education—Take your children places. What do I mean? Take them to other people's houses, to stores, to restaurants, to airports. These are places where important interactions with others, especially adults, can take place. I know some people who don't take their children anywhere. One parent always stays home with the kids, and the other goes out. These children get little interaction with others, especially other adults. Oftentimes you can tell who these children are. They are the ones who either turn away, or don't answer you at all when you say hello. Yes, there are some children who are just shy, and I acknowledge that my theory is not true for everyone. But, the earlier your children begin interacting with the world, the earlier their life education will begin, and the better prepared they will be for the life ahead of them.

Gail, the mother of adult children offers this:

Take your children with you when you volunteer. My kids went with me when I did Meals on Wheels, which was their only significant exposure to older people since their grandparents lived far away.

School Education—Classroom education is a no-brainer. Everyone knows how this works. Study, get good grades, go to college or other post-secondary schooling, and get a good job. While we know how it works, it's not always that easy. Make sure you are involved with your children's education. Unless you have exceptional children, they will need help along the way with homework and studying for tests. I encourage you to share this responsibility with your spouse. I am relearning a lot of things these days, from geography to math, from spelling to social studies. Helping your children with their homework is one of your most important jobs as a dad. Make their homework a priority in *your* day.

Politeness and Courtesy

Two phrases our children must be black-belt proficient in are please and thank you. I am always impressed with young children who are able to use these words without prompting from their parents. If we dads do our part in teaching good manners to our children, maybe one day it won't be impressive to see children exhibit good manners, it will be the norm. As with many things, I firmly believe politeness is learned behavior.

How are *your* manners?

Teaching the Value of Money

Living in the capitalist society as we do, it is hard to ignore how big of a part money plays in everyday life. The earlier our children begin to understand money and finance, the better prepared they will be. In a world with endless toys and other stuff (Kate hates when I call it junk) to buy, Beth and I are trying to emphasize the importance of giving.

In our house Emily and Kate each earn allowance for performing daily activities and chores. They also have the opportunity to earn bonuses through excellent behavior and for extra help around the house. They keep track of their activity using charts that Beth I put together and post in the kitchen.

Before School	Monday	Tuesday	Wednesday	Thursday	Friday	Saturday	Sunday
Brush Teeth	x	x					
Make Bed	x	x					
Lunch in Backpack	x	x					
Eat Breakfast	x	x					
Homework Signed	x	x					
After School							
Take out Garbage	x						
Homework	x						
Practice Violin	x						
Set dinner table	x						
Pajamas	x						
Brush Teeth	x						
Read before bed	x						

Whatever allowance they earn is divided three ways: 1) Give, 2) Save, 3) Spend. We focus our teaching on giving and saving, and #3 seems to take care of itself.

I know a dad who pays his children for grades they earn in school. He explains to them that one of his fatherhood responsibilities is to earn money for the family through having a job. Their job is to attend school, study, and earn good grades. Just as he is compensated for performance and not just showing up, they too are compensated more for better grades. It is a great illustrator of cause and affect, teaching children that they control their own destiny in life through the choices they make.

Whatever allowance/reward system you decide is right for your family, make sure to teach your children that giving to others and saving for the future (I could write an entire book called *Delayed Gratification in an I-Want-Everything-Now World*) is simply the right thing.

Honesty

One of the most important aspects to having integrity is honesty. Teach your children early that honesty at all times is not recommended—it's required.

As I discuss throughout this book, this starts with the example we, as dads, set. You may never see the results of your teaching first hand, but here is a story from our family.

Emily was in second grade, and they were doing time tests in her class. You probably remember doing them as a child. One hundred problems (addition or subtraction in second grade) on a sheet of paper, and one minute to see how many you can complete correctly. Emily desperately wanted to keep up with the other students in her class, and also reach the goal her teacher had given her. She could get to thirty-two, but not thirty-five. One day the teacher said "time," which meant stop and put your pencil down. This day Emily decided to do a few more problems, after the buzzer. No one noticed, and the day went on as it normally does. The one thing that was different was how Emily felt inside. She knew what she did was not right. When she walked through the door at home that day I said, "How was your day, Buddy?" Her first words were, "I cheated in math, Dad." It had been eating away at her all day, and I could tell she was relieved to tell me. She *knew* she had done something dishonest, and it didn't feel right. In this situation, a child feeling guilty is a good thing. It's the way they should feel. At that moment, I couldn't have been more proud of her. She wrote a note to her teacher, explaining what happened, and her teacher allowed her to take the test again.

Honesty was something we had discussed with Emily and Kate, and it was gratifying to see the concept had sunk in.

Choices

In their book, *Putting Family First*, authors Barbara Carlson and William Doherty suggest allowing your children to participate in one activity at a time. Their feeling, which I agree with 100 percent, is that we have lost much of the important connecting time with our children due to crazy schedules in which multiple children in the family are in multiple activities.

Our family tries to adhere to this one-activity-at-a-time notion, and Emily's one activity is violin lessons. When she was nine years old she wanted to quit, citing the fact that it was getting too hard as her primary reason. While we allowed her to present her full case, both verbally and written, as to why she wanted to quit, Beth and I decided it was not in her best interest to let her do so. She's wasn't happy with us, but that wasn't an important part of the equation. I know that we made a decision for her that will benefit her in the long run, and it's our responsibility to help her learn to make good choices.

My feeling is that our current culture is one that coddles children too much, concerned more with keeping them happy instead of doing what's most beneficial to their growth and development. It seems like there aren't enough absolutes anymore. Some parents try to justify and allow questionable behavior, rather than put their foot down. In this crazy, hurry up world we live in, parents sometimes are just too tired for the fight, and it's easier just to give in.

In his book, *No, Why Kids—of All ages—Need to Hear it and Ways Parents Can Say It*, Dr. David Walsh talks about the yes world we are living in. He says that disappointment and emotional pain are a part of the world we live in, and everyone, adults and children, need to learn how to deal with them. With regard to children he says, "Don't we want them to develop virtues like perseverance, patience, commitment, determination, and diligence? These virtues don't come automatically; kids have to learn them. And the lessons are not always easy or pleasant."

One of the most difficult but important aspects to parenting is helping our children learn to make good choices, and the good choice is not always the easy choice.

God Bless the USA

While your children will learn the history of our great nation through textbooks and teachers at school, I challenge you to be the one to instill a sense of patriotism. We live in a great time of divide between the two major political parties, where many people are at extreme ends of the spectrum. I strongly feel we need to move towards the center of the debate and find ways for liberals and conservatives to work together. Because this is a book about fathers and not politics, I will cut my political commentary short.

Regardless of what party you endorse (if any), teach your children that we are extremely fortunate to live in the United States of America. There is no other country like ours on the planet. People from other parts of the world literally die to get into our country. They don't take for granted the incredible opportunities we have. From freedom of speech to freedom of religion, you can be who you want, and do want you want in the "Nifty Fifty." Teach your children to respect the ideals that our nation stands for. Here are a few more ideas:

1. **Display a flag at your house.**

2. **Remind your children why we celebrate President's Day, Memorial Day, Independence Day, and other national holidays.**

3. **During the national anthem, respect and salute the flag, and teach your children that it's not acceptable or appropriate to goof around during the playing of the anthem. Too many people have sacrificed too many things, including those who have died for our freedoms, to not pay respectful attention.**

4. **Vote, and take your children with you to the polls.**

Reinforce the civic lessons your child is learning in school with home lessons of your own. President George W. Bush was giving his State of the Union address to the nation. I was in my office working, and Emily (ten years old at the time) was watching a kids' show in the family room. I decided to seize the moment and explain to her what the State of the Union was all about. We turned the channel to see the president delivering his address, and after my brief explanation, I returned to my office, assuming Emily would change the channel back to what she'd been watching. About twenty minutes later I called her to come upstairs, brush her teeth and get ready for bed. She quickly responded, "Come on, Dad, I'm watching the State of the Union, can't I stay up a little longer?"

Chapter Review:

- One of our duties as parents is to help our children maneuver through the many images and ideals presented to them, and determine which are important, and equally importantly, which aren't.
- We can't teach our children everything—nor should we want to.
- Focus your attention on those things that are important to your family. Teach them lessons that help them understand the world.
- Teach them lessons that help them deal with the noise— television, Internet, magazines, video games, as well as other children and adults.
- Help them create a value system that appreciates inner qualities like honesty, integrity, and helping others, while placing less importance on things like physical beauty and material possessions.

FOCUS

Care More Than Anyone Else
Leading By Example

Stand for Something

If your friends were asked to say one thing about you to describe who you are, what would they say?

Some men feel as though they are defined by their jobs. In past generations this was certainly true. Oftentimes, men would join a company out of college, and work there for thirty-five to forty years before retiring.

My father-in-law worked for the same company for thirty-eight years, his only post-college job, and retired in 2004. It took a while for him to get used to introducing himself using only his name, rather than his name followed by his company's name. After nearly four decades of association, being an employee of that company was part of the fabric of who he was.

Our generation is far less likely to spend that much time at one employer, and, therefore, most of us won't ever be defined by whom we work for. With that said, how do you define who you are? I think it is a direct result of what you feel most passionately. For instance, I am passionate about my family. I hope those who know me well think of me first as a devoted husband and father. In my mind this defines who I am. It is what I stand for, first and foremost.

I want to be clear that there is nothing wrong with being known as a hard worker with a successful career. Strive to be known as someone with a great work ethic, who finds a way to balance work and family.

Do the Right Thing

I was recently visiting one of my favorite clients in the Twin Cities. As I got out of my car, I found a $20 bill on the parking lot. I looked around to see if there was anyone else around, and there wasn't. I don't know if it makes a difference for the story, but understand that I found the money in a *bank* parking lot. While most places of business involve money, a bank's business *is* money.

When I met with my client, I explained to him what happened and told him I wasn't sure what to do. Should I turn it in to the lost and found? Does a bank have a lost and found? Would someone actually come in to the *bank* and say, "I lost $20, have you seen it?" His advice was swift and simple. "Put it in the offering plate at church." My first thought *was why didn't I think of that*? My second thought was, *this will be a great example for Emily and Kate*. When in doubt, give. I went home, told them what happened, and put that "Jackson" in the offering plate on Sunday. I hope the story sticks with them.

By the way, if you lost $20 on Wednesday, July 24, 2005, at the Wells Fargo Bank parking lot in Apple Valley, Minnesota, now you know where your $20 went.

Get Involved

Have you ever volunteered in a classroom? Have you ever volunteered to be a coach? Have you ever volunteered to be chaperone on a field trip or a church retreat? If you are answering yes to any of these, I applaud you loudly. Not only is this a chance to experience more of life with your own child, but whether or not you realize it, you are now given the opportunity to positively influence many more children.

I am fortunate to have fulfilled all of the aforementioned roles, and have thoroughly enjoyed each of them. I have felt a great sense of purpose as a volunteer. I know you will feel the same way if you choose your attitude correctly. Don't approach volunteering with young children as baby sitting. Instead, remember that you might be the one person that day that makes a child feel good about himself/

herself. You might be the one person that day who makes them feel loved and accepted. Many children have struggles at home.

I challenge you to be a positive influence. Regardless of how busy you think you are, *get involved*.

Making a Difference

Children are never too young to learn the importance of giving for the benefit of others. Beth's brother was diagnosed in the fall of 2002 with type 1 diabetes. He was thirty-five at the time, in excellent physical condition, and there was no family history of diabetes. While still wondering why this had happened to her brother, Beth decided to organize a group to participate in the American Diabetes Association Walk for Diabetes. This event takes place every year in dozens of cities throughout the country. Like other charitable events, people make donations to individuals or teams.

A few extra-inspiring things occurred during the 2005 walk at the Metrodome in Minneapolis, Minnesota. The first was the fact that the Minnesota walk raised significantly more money than the year before. This, in a year where people were already giving to the relief efforts of a Tsunami in Indonesia, and two devastating hurricanes in the United States (Katrina and Rita).

Perhaps the most inspirational aspect to the walk was who the top individual fund raiser was. A nine-year-old from southern Minnesota raised over $73,000! I can only imagine how proud his parents were. Real, live proof there is no such thing as too young when it comes to making a difference through volunteering and giving.

Another story from 2005 is about two brothers, eight and five years old. They decided to have a joint birthday party, inviting twenty-one friends. Instead of bringing presents for the boys, they asked their guests to bring toys that would be donated to less fortunate children during the holiday season. How amazing is that! Kids giving up birthday presents to help other kids.

Remember, the children are our future. Teach them well and let them lead the way.

Hope

"What you do you want to be when you grow up?" We were all asked that question as children, and our children are being asked that question as well. If your children are anything like mine, the answer will change several times. At one point Emily wanted to be a nurse, doctor, and airport worker (we're still not sure if that meant she wanted to be a pilot, or run the snack-shack on concourse C), all at the same time. The one thing we were sure never to tell her was she couldn't do all those simultaneously. Never take away your child's hope. Hope is good. Hope leads to dreams and dreams lead to goals.

Having hope allows children to believe all things are possible, when adult logic might say it isn't. Never steal your children's hope.

Chapter Review:

- Whose behavior is your child modeling? Someone on TV? Other children?
- Make sure that you are the number one role model for your children and that they want to grow up to be like you.
- Pray that other adults like teachers, coaches, and friends' parents have a positive influence on your children.
- But, take great care in being the one to instill the important values that will shape them for a lifetime.
- Lead by example, and live a life worth emulating.

FOC**U**S

Undivided Attention
Be Present—Stay Connected

Quantity and Quality

Quality time has become a common phrase for many dads explaining time spent with their children. I'd like to respectfully offer the idea that *quality time* is not possible without *quantity time*. In fact, the whole FOCUSed Father message rests on this concept.

Our greatest gift to our children is our time, and I feel we show our love and commitment to them through giving them large amounts of that time. Not that quality time is completely invalid. In fact, I would describe quality time as the connecting aspect to FOCUSed fatherhood. Remember, it really isn't important to children what you are doing with them. What is paramount to them is that you are around and present on a frequent basis.

I don't have a lot of detailed memories of my early childhood. But, what I do remember is that my dad was around most of the time. The positive memories I do have are not about doing something specific with him. Rather, the memories are about him simply being there often, providing love, guidance, and a sense of security.

Be there for your children, and "there" is wherever your children are.

"Getting Love From My Dad"

I was talking to Kate between appointments, and decided to do some research for the book. I asked her, "What is the best thing about your dad?" I smiled widely when she gave the answer, "Getting love from my dad." When I asked the question, that's the type of answer I was hoping for. If she had said, "Because he buys me things," I think I would have never written this book. To make sure that's how she truly felt, I asked a follow-up question. "What's better: going to the Mall of America (there is actually an amusement park there, for those who haven't experienced the world's largest mall), going swimming, going to Chuck E Cheese, or getting love from your Dad?" "Can I have three answers?" was her response. After telling her she could only pick one, her answer again was "Getting love from my dad," but was quickly followed up by an amended response, "Getting love from my dad at the Mall of America."

I love going to parks and restaurants with the kids, but I don't want only to be the fun dad. Children don't need fathers for playmates. They need us for love, guidance, and direction. Do you know any dads who barely spend time with their children during the workweek, then take them everywhere on Saturday and Sunday—The Weekend Dad? Fatherhood is *not* a weekend event.

As I said, I enjoy going places with Emily and Kate. But Kate's response about getting love tells me that if we weren't able to do those things, she would still be happy. More importantly, she would feel my love. For in some way, although she was only five years old when she said those words, I knew she understood that she loves me not because we do fun things together, but because I am actively involved her life on a daily basis.

What Kids Really Want

When I told Emily, who was eight at the time, that I wanted to write a book about fatherhood, she asked, "Why?" After giving her an answer that apparently wasn't good enough, she ran upstairs to her room. I followed her up to see what was going through her complex, eight-year-old mind. When I asked her what was wrong, she burst into tears and said, "I'm afraid that if you write a book, you won't be the same dad." I assured her that I would always be the same dad, and if I ever was fortunate enough to write books as my full time occupation I'd actually be around even more. With that, Emily's world was once again in order.

The interaction reminded me that children don't dream about having famous parents or attaining wealth and status. Children simply want their parents to be there, providing security, love, and normalcy in a world that tends to be insecure and abnormal.

As for me, I continue striving to be the same dad.

The World Does Not Revolve Around Your Schedule

Scott is the father of two boys, and shares a great story about seizing the moment with his seven-year-old.

I got home about 6:00 p.m. Monday after I had stopped and given plasma at the blood center, and was a little tired from the day at work and the blood-letting. After I joined the dinner already in progress and finished up, Trevor asked if we could go do some stuff. As much as I wanted to sit on the couch under a blanket, I said, "Sure," and we went up to his room to play some board games, then into the office so he could show me a cool racing game on the Hot Wheels website (which he beat me at every time), and then back into his room to read books and have a snack before lights out. After his teeth were brushed, I was tucking him into bed when he looked at me and said, "Thanks for playing with me, Dad. You're a really cool guy. I love you."

Does fatherhood get more rewarding? That's a HUGE reward for an hour or so of my time.

Crazy Daddy-Daughter Time

Today at the Berg house we had M&Ms for breakfast, wore clothes that didn't match, and didn't brush our hair until the afternoon. In our family, we refer to this as "crazy daddy-daughter time." (a phrase I have borrowed from one of the best motivational/inspirational speakers/artists I have met, Erik Wahl—www.erikwahl.com).

Rules and structure provide the foundation for order and organization in any family's house. They give boundaries, create norms, and provide a sense of security. While I advocate living by the rules most of the time (my parents will tell you I was a rule follower), I also think that every once in a while rules must be broken.

Have you ever eaten dessert first? Have you ever had Cocoa Puffs for dinner? Have you ever run in the sprinklers with your clothes on? Kids need to know that flexibility is an important part of life. Flexibility will be necessary in marriage, at work, and in social settings throughout their lifetimes. I'm sure you know someone right now who always needs to have it their way. Maybe it's a co-worker, maybe it's a family member, or maybe it's even your spouse (just for the record, that comment is *not* directed at Beth). While not being able to actually prove it to you, I'll bet they were rarely, if ever, allowed to stretch the rules growing up.

Have clear cut rules in your family. But, every once in a while break the rules together as a family.

School Starts Tomorrow

As I write this, school starts tomorrow for Emily and Kate. I know everyone says this, but I am wondering where the time has gone.

I was with another dad yesterday who has a two-year-old. I looked at her picture, and tried to imagine Emily at that age. It was both hard and easy to remember her. At times like this I remind myself to embrace the passage of time and changes that come with it, rather than lament about how fast life is going. With our children, every age brings different experiences, challenges, and joys. Remember, it's those life experiences that have shaped who we are as adults. I urge you not to spend time wishing they were two years old again, or wishing for them to be older. Live in the moment. Seize the day. I heard a great quote regarding parenthood from NFL coach Herman Edwards. He was addressing a group of parents, urging them to make their children a priority and said, "Your life is not a dress rehearsal."

Focus on the present, because that is all that is promised to us. Your child needs you today. Be present, and in the present, because before you know it, school starts tomorrow.

Protect, Don't Shelter

As mentioned earlier, Hurricane Katrina was one of the worst natural disasters in the history of our great nation. The stories, pictures, and video that came from New Orleans and regions affected were, at times, unfathomable. People drowned, starved to death, were raped, murdered, and robbed. The horror caused me to have some of the same feelings I did on 9/11 regarding the question of how much of this do we expose to our young children.

I believe children should know there was a terrible storm, and many people were hurt, and some even died. There is no point in pretending that it didn't happened. This was real, just as 9/11 was real. By the time you read this, we may have experienced another disaster—perhaps another hurricane, a major earthquake, or, God forbid, another major terror attack. Our children's lifetime will be filled with these types of events, and they need to know how to process the information that will come to them. Should we give them gory details about how people died, how many people, etc.? Probably not. Speak to them in basic terms they can understand. And, don't forget to tell them all the good that can come out of tragedy. Tell them about the heroes who saved people from drowning in their homes. Tell them about the people who opened their homes to those whose homes were destroyed by the hurricane. And tell them they can help. Have them donate part of their allowance to The Red Cross or another relief organization. Take them to the store and buy supplies that are being requested (blankets, clothes, toiletries, etc.).

With the ever-present media covering every event in real time, your kids are going to be exposed to crisis after crisis. Teach them that while we can't prevent most tragedies, we can most certainly help those affected by them.

Patience

It was Sunday night and I was the lone parent in our house. Beth had a girl's weekend away, so it was just me, Emily and Kate (and the puppy—which as many of you know, is like having another child). For reasons I'm not sure, my patience with Emily and Kate was very short this evening. For that I was very disappointed in myself. It would be one thing if they had been fighting the whole time, but they were simply being kids, which means they didn't do everything I asked them first time, or remember to throw every wrapper away. They committed no serious crimes, but I spoke to them as though they had been going 80 mph in 50 mph zone. Rather than work through minor incidents in ways that would teach and instruct, I chose to elevate the situations quickly by barking at the kids.

I am now reminding myself that many things in our lives are out of our control. The behavior our children exhibit at times definitely falls in that category. I was the guy who swore his children would never throw a fit in Target. That's funny. What makes us better fathers is how we choose to handle things not in our control. We need to rise above other things on our minds (work, money, etc.) and give our children the patience and understanding they deserve.

Sassy Dad

Pick your battles. Don't sweat the small stuff. You've probably heard these sayings before. A few days ago I was trying to get the kids to go upstairs to brush their teeth, then get in bed. I would follow a few minutes later to tuck them in. This is the normal bedtime routine at our house, and I'm sure you have or will have your own bedtime rituals. I had said no to Kate a few times that evening, and I'm not even sure what the issues were. I had to raise my voice a little to get her to start walking toward the stairs. She stopped, looked at me, and shouted, "You're not letting me do anything I want. You're being all sassy, Dad!" In a split second I had to decide how to react to this obviously inappropriate behavior. My first thought was to ground her for about five years. My second thought was *what exactly is a sassy dad*? Anyway, I scolded her, pointing out that it was simply not acceptable for her to speak to me this way. She headed upstairs to her bed crying and waited for me come up.

Before going upstairs I thought about whether or not to punish her in some way. While I thought she was way out of line, I decided her response came mostly from being tired and feeling a little under the weather. This outburst on her part is not a pattern. Given these factors, I decided not to press charges and dropped the incident.

Remember, not everything is worth an inquisition. Pick your battles, and allow yourself some flexibility.

Still wondering what a sassy dad is.

Drugs

After a late October round of golf, a good friend clued me in about the realities of drugs in high schools. We were talking about the issues we face as parents as our kids get older. His oldest son was a fifteen-year-old freshman at the time. I was astonished to learn how prevalent marijuana is. In one of his classes, the teacher at the high school asked the class, "How many of you know someone that smokes marijuana?" About 70 percent of the hands went up. The follow-up question was "How many of you know where to go if you want to buy drugs?" One hundred percent of the hands went up. **One hundred percent!** This terrifies me, but fortunately I have a few years to prepare.

While being terrified, I am encouraged by the proactive approach many school districts are taking to prepare young children for the drug and alcohol decisions they will face. Emily's fifth grade class participated in the local D.A.R.E. program (Drug Abuse Resistance Education). For three months they learned about the dangers of drugs and alcohol from a local police officer. At the end of the program students made a pledge never to do drugs, and a graduation ceremony, with many parents in attendance, was held in the gymnasium.

The D.A.R.E. program provides an excellent platform for many conversations at home about the perils of drugs and alcohol. Regardless if your children are exposed to a program like this, you need to talk openly about drugs and the consequences of using them, starting at an early age. The bottom line for us to communicate is that drug addiction ruins lives—the abuser's and those who care about them.

Tell your kids that drugs are wrong and will not be tolerated in your family. You must deliver this message. You must deliver it early, and you must deliver it over and over.

Visit www.abovetheinfluence.com with your children for more information on dealing with the drug issue.

The Expedition

When Emily was about five years old, Beth and the kids were riding in the car with good family friends of ours. At the time, they had two children about the same age as ours. In fact, Emily and Jacob were born only five weeks apart. As the story goes (I wasn't in the van), there was a heated discussion occurring between Emily and Jacob. From the back of the minivan, nearly in tears, Jacob said, "Mom, will you please tell Emily that an expedition is a very long journey." Apparently Emily was arguing, also correctly, that an Expedition was the Ford-made SUV that passed them a few minutes ago. That's my girl. You see, I am somewhat of a car freak. I like to look at them, talk about them, drive them, and much to Beth's dismay, buy them too often. At an early age, Emily joined the vehicle lovers club. She was able to identify makes and models of vehicles, and even noticed differences in small things like the wheel designs. While I can't say for sure, I don't think Jakob has the same knowledge of, and passion for, vehicles. He is, however, and has always been, extremely intelligent. He knew what an expedition was.

The point of this story is your children will emulate you, whether you want them to or not. I did not set out to teach Emily all about cars. But, because I have been present in Emily's life from an early age, she emulates me in certain ways. My advice to you is to live a life worth emulating.

Self-Fulfilling Prophecies

During one of our parent-teacher conferences, Emily received high praise from her teacher. While this wasn't a surprise to us, it is always rewarding to hear others, especially teachers, speak well of your children. For the past few years math has been challenging for Emily. For me it falls under the theory that most of us are strong either in English or math. At some point a few years ago, Emily began struggling with some new concepts and self-labeled herself as not good in math. I think she now approaches math with that belief in her mind. Before even attempting a new problem or concept, she is at a psychological disadvantage. She has always done well in spelling and reading and, therefore, has a high degree of confidence in those subjects. Her attitude propels her to success in those areas and hinders her ability to excel in math. I truly believe that half the battle is how she views her abilities.

Henry Ford once said, "Whether you think you can do a thing or not, you are probably right." Keep this in mind as you interact with your children. Help them *see* success, rather than failure.

Consistency

Aside from spending time with Beth, Emily, and Kate, there are few things I would rather be doing than golfing. From the "my time" on my priorities list, it is the thing I love most. For those of you bitten with the golf bug, you know the pure joy *and* heartache the game gives you. One day you've got it figured out, and the next day it's as though you have never picked up a club in your entire life. While I have played the game for more than twenty-five years, my game has improved significantly over the last five years. One of the keys to my improvement was a series of lessons I took three years ago. For the first time in my life I learned about the technical aspects to the golf swing. I was video taped and my swing was analyzed against some of the PGA Tour players (a humbling experience). Armed with a new understanding of what I was *supposed* to do, I set out to improve my game through practice. It took a while to feel comfortable with some of the changes my teacher made to my swing, but eventually it became more natural. I am not always able to execute the proper swing, but at least I now understand what has gone wrong when the balls goes where I don't intend it to go.

Perhaps this is a little like fatherhood. Hopefully you're gaining some insight from this book. Maybe you've read other parenting books. You know what the right moves are. Now it's a matter of execution. When faced with a teaching moment, will you teach? When faced with a leadership opportunity, will you lead? When asked to simply be there, will you? My advice is that you practice great fatherhood technique by welcoming these opportunities. Your dedication to executing in these situations will help shape the future of your children. The good news here is that consistent fathering is much easier than consistent golf.

Six Ideas for Staying Connected

1. Read

One of the greatest habits we can help our children create is the need to read. Countless good things come from reading to our children, and then, as they get older, having them read to us. Obviously, reading is a crucial life skill that will impact and affect our children throughout their entire lives. In our family, we have designated the thirty minutes before going to bed as reading time. Some nights we read to them, some nights they read to themselves, and some nights they read to us. I remember when Kate was in first grade, which is the first year in our district that kids learn to read. One night she said to me, "Dad, I want to read to you." It had been a few weeks since she read anything to me. What a difference two weeks makes. She read, nearly flawlessly, four books to me.

The ability of children to learn and retain great amounts of information is amazing. Watching them develop life skills like reading is even more amazing. We have made reading a high-value activity in our house, and it appears to be having the intended effect.

2. Family Dinners

I will be the first one to say that sitting down with your family for dinner every night of every week is simply not possible for most families. I will, however, suggest you make a point to have a family dinner, at your dinner table, sometime each week. Many productive and rewarding things happen through family dinners.

It might be one of the only times your family will have each other's undivided attention. Having meaningful conversations is crucial to your relationship with your children. The dinner table provides an excellent forum for these conversations. Dinner gatherings also provide an opportunity to find out what happened in everyone's day. What was good about school? How was the math test? What's coming up tomorrow? For some dads, dinner time is the first time during the day they see their kids. Use this time wisely. When I talk to parents whose children have recently gone to college, one thing they always say is, "The dinner table sure is quiet. I miss those times."

Remember, a family meal doesn't have to happen at home. Eating out counts too. In fact, as long as you are together somewhere eating, it's a family dinner. Beth's current work schedule has her working until about 8:00 p.m. on Thursdays. We have created a family ritual over the last year where we bring dinner to her, creating another family meal.

3. Bedtime Rituals

For some parents, bedtime with young children can be the most challenging part of the day. One thing that has not changed over the generations is that most kids, when given the choice, just don't want to go to bed. What has changed is some of the distractions today's world gives us. In the absence of limits set by parents, things like television, the Internet, and video games can keep our children from getting the sleep they need. They might also prevent meaningful interactions, like reading and storytelling with fathers and mothers.

The key to a smoother end to the day is having a bedtime ritual, where the same schedule is followed every night. Children thrive on structure even at an early age. I remember when Emily went to preschool with a class of about twenty other three-year-olds. A few weeks after school started, Beth called me after dropping in mid-way through class with a surprising report. She said that all the kids were behaving and doing exactly what the teacher wanted them to do. Did I mention that it was *twenty three-year-olds?* The key, it turns out, is that the teacher had established a routine that was followed each day.

Structure is good, and when we adults provide it, acting out bedtime seems to be less of a problem. Have your children help create their own bedtime rituals, and it just may end up being their favorite time of the day.

4. Dream List

Have you made a dream list for yourself? Are you wondering what a dream list is? Here is the idea: Write down one hundred things you want to do in your lifetime. Maybe you want to visit all fifty states. Maybe you want to skydive. Maybe you want to meet the Pope. Whatever your dreams are, write them down.

Once you have done this for yourself, if your children are old enough, have them do the same exercise (they might not get to one hundred and that's okay). This will give you an excellent chance to find out what your kids are thinking. Plus you'll be teaching something I think is very healthy, which is to have dreams for the future.

Goals and dreams are not the same. As I discussed earlier, set goals for things you know you can accomplish through following a predetermined plan. Have dreams for things you may, or may not, be able to realize. For instance, one of my goals is to pay for Emily and Kate's college education. I have a plan for this, and if I stick to the plan, I will accomplish my goal. On the other hand, I have a dream to meet Oprah Winfrey some day (hopefully to talk about this book, and FOCUSed Father). However, it's really out of my control, as to whether she wants to meet me, and, therefore, I can't develop a plan. Many of the great people in history, including Oprah, dared to dream. Walt Disney had a dream and has brought joy to millions all over the world.

So, make your list, help your children make theirs, and dream big dreams.

Use this space to get started.

Dream List

_____

_____

_____

_____

_____

_____

_____

_____

_____

_____

_____

_____

_____

_____

_____

_____

_____

_____

5. Touch

I firmly believe, and countless studies show, that physical closeness is vital to our children's development. Traditionally, this role has been filled by women in our culture. We dads need to change that. One of the greatest things we can teach our children is how to love others. Teach your children to love through words _and_ actions. I spoke at one of the local school district's parenting forums, and a father told me how he has always hugged his son. He felt as though it was an important part of the strong connection they had, and even though his son was a senior in high school, they still hugged frequently.

Hold them close now. As those who have fathered before us say, time goes by fast.

6. Games

Beth and I both grew up playing games in our families, and we are carrying the tradition on with Emily and Kate. Games serve many purposes, including teaching, connecting, and simply having fun.

Games can be played anywhere and anytime. They might involve a board, cards, dice, or just an imagination. Obviously, the age of your children has a lot to do with the kinds of games you play. At a young age you might start playing pattycake. As you children get older, card games and board games are introduced. One of the simple games I have played with our children for several years is called "This or That." All this game consists of is asking one another to choose a preference from two things. Colors, foods, television shows are examples of common topics. Pink or purple? Chicken or pizza? *Hannah Montana* or *That's So Raven*? I get great pleasure in watching them agonize over the decision, because they have to choose one over the other. This is also a good bedtime activity. I do this with Emily and Kate at the end of reading time, just before lights out. Imagine what you can learn about your children through this simple question game.

Turn off the television and play games.

Connecting When You Are Not Physically Present

To this point I have made only a few references to situations where you don't live full time with your children. With the divorce rate hovering around 50 percent in this country, there are millions of dads in this situation. Although that is not my personal situation, I used to do a good deal of traveling for business, and had to focus on being there when not actually present. I feel strongly about using every possible tool to stay connected when you are not actually with your children. Here are some ideas to stay connected:

Cell phones—No matter where you are, make every effort to check in a minimum of three times a day—morning, after school, and bedtime.

Email or text messaging—Email your children frequently, taking advantage of technology.

Notes—Leave notes for your children before you leave on trips.

Webcams—This technology has become much easier and less expensive.

Always attend school and extracurricular functions—Even if you don't live with your children full time due to divorce, their concerts, recitals, D.A.R.E graduation, soccer games, etc. should be a priority for you—your presence will be even more meaningful if this is your situation.

The website www.fathers.com provides some excellent ideas for divorced dads to stay connected with their children.

Chapter Review:

- We live in a world today with many things competing for our attention.
- Regardless of how crazy you think your life might be, always make time to give your children undivided attention. This is time where nothing else matters more than what your children have to say.
- Turn off the TV, cell phone, and PDA, and connect with them through conversations and games.

FOCU<u>S</u>

Say "I Love You"
Don't Underestimate the Power of Your Words

Positive Communication

Your children's future is full of promise. Make sure they know that. Too often our children's world is one of "if you don't..."

- If you don't eat your vegetables, you won't grow.
- If you don't get good grades, you won't go to college.
- If you don't brush your teeth, they will rot.
- If you don't clean your room, you'll be in trouble.

I suggest a world of "if you..."

- If you work hard in school, you can be anything you want.
- If you are kind to other people, you will find others treat you in the same way.
- If you help others less fortunate, you will have a sense of fulfillment and purpose in life.

Without a doubt, this is something I learned from my dad (and from my mom for that matter, but since this is a book for dads...). As I mentioned in the introduction, I am blessed to have a father who has always had a positive outlook on life. I never once heard, "you can't do that." My father always encouraged and motivated me in positive ways, and I am convinced that greatly impacted my view on the world and life, which is one of great optimism and hope.

I recently had lunch with a client of mine. This particular individual is someone who has crossed the line from just being a client and is someone I consider a friend. When we get together we spend most of our time talking about non-business-related things like our kids and triathlons. This day the subject of accomplishment came up. He said he never really feels totally content because he often feels like whatever he does, it's not enough. I asked him where he thought that belief came from. Without hesitating he said it came from his childhood and his parents. While not condemning his parents, he recalls only being acknowledged for negatives. He got very good grades in school, but was never praised for them. Instead of being praised for the four As, he was questioned about the one B. This is just one example of how much of an impact we have on our children and how long that impact lasts.

Make an effort to spend more time encouraging and praising, and less time discouraging and criticizing. There is a well known poem by Dorothy Law Nolte called *Children Learn What They Live* that illustrates this point (the poem is easily found with a simple Internet search).

Conversations, Part I

During one of the parenting classes Beth and I participated in at our church, Pastor Steve wrote down the word conversations on the white board. The ensuing discussion was about when you have conversations, where you have conversations, and how you have conversations with your children. This really got me thinking. On a daily basis, how often am I having meaningful conversations with Emily and Kate? A definition of conversation would be useful here: The Random House dictionary defines conversation as "oral communication between persons." Notice how it is "*between* persons." I don't believe the following interaction qualifies as a conversation: "How was school today, Emily?' "Fine, Dad." Notice how I am doing most of the talking? In order to have meaningful conversations, which is something dads need to do, we need to ask thought provoking questions. A few questions I like:

- What was your favorite part of school today?
- What are you most looking forward to this summer?

- What was the most exciting or unusual thing that happened today?

I think many days go by for some children without them being asked these types of questions. When Emily was in third grade volleyball, Beth coached the team, and I served as her assistant. During one of our games, when the kids rotated out, I started asking them the "favorite part of school today" question. Most of them looked at me with an expression that said, "What?" I don't think most of them had been routinely asked the question. For the record, they were a great bunch of girls who appeared to have great parents. By the second time they rotated out, they were full of answers about their day at school. The bottom line is to engage your children every single day in meaningful conversation. You will be amazed at what you learn. By the way, we didn't win too many games that year. Maybe my line of questioning distracted them from the task at hand.

Conversations, Part II

During the same parenting class, Pastor Steve gave us a story about the consequences of not having meaningful, frequent conversations with your children. Several years ago he had a member of the church he was serving approach him and ask this question, "Will you please tell me about my daughter?" While he had been active in his son's life, primarily through sports, he had not done the same with his daughter (the youngest child), missing opportunities for meaningful conversations. All of a sudden his daughter was sixteen, and he didn't know who she was. Think about that for a moment, he didn't know *who* she was. He didn't know her friends, her favorite school subject, or what her dreams for the future were. How profoundly sad.

Don't put off conversation, trivial or important, with your child.

Conversations Without Your Children

While an ongoing dialogue with your children is vital to their growth and your relationship with them, be mindful that some conversations are not meant for their ears.

Although I strive to be non-judgmental of others, I know there are conversations Beth and I have where we might say things critical of others. In a perfect world we would never say less than flattering things about other people and the lives they lead, but you and I both know we don't live in a perfect world.

Conversations about adult matters should be kept out of earshot of our children. I believe children are like sponges. They soak up everything they hear, and then, when we least expect it, they spill it out to us or others. My experience has been that Emily and Kate understand things a lot sooner than I expect. I have learned that through the questions they have asked me regarding something they heard Beth and I discussing.

Colorful language is another area we can all improve in. In 2000, we had our first experience building a home. The home turned out great, but the building process was somewhat of a nightmare. We worked with a small builder who was lacking any sense of customer service. Beth and I left many heated messages on the builder's voicemail during the six-month (supposed to be four) process—*only* messages because he never returned our calls. A few months after moving in, Emily (about four at the time) responded to a question Beth asked her with, "What in the hell for?" Obviously she didn't pick that up on her own. We were certain that it came as a result of our words toward the builder, and, although pretty harmless, it serves as a good example of the sponge theory I mentioned earlier.

The message here is simple: Have adult conversations only in presence of adults.

Three Words That Mean Everything

In my opinion the three most important words you can expose your children to are "I love you." Say them often. Children not only need to feel a father's love through actions, but also through the spoken word. My parents both told me frequently that they loved me throughout my childhood, and that continues to this day. I make a point to tell Emily and Kate multiple times every day that I love them. I'll ask them, "Do you know how much I love you?" This will often result in an argument about who loves whom more. A few days ago I said to Emily, "I am bigger, so I have more love to give." She thought for second and said, "You got me there, Dad."

I told the girls about a client of mine who went to Louisiana over Thanksgiving to volunteer. He and his family helped feed seven hundred people Thanksgiving dinner, and then worked on rebuilding houses devastated by Hurricanes Katrina and Rita. When I asked the girls if they would like to do something like that, Kate said, "I would love to do that, Dad!" Then she offered this: "Hey, Dad, we could go there for Valentine's Day because that's for love."

Talk about love in your house. Tell your children you love them. It will help them feel love and understand love.

Chapter Review:

- Do not underestimate the power of your words.
- Our children need to hear that they are special and that we are proud of them.
- Positive verbal reinforcement should be done loudly and often.
- Try to praise more (in public) and criticize less (in private).
- Your words will stick with your children for the rest of their lives.
- Don't let a day go by without telling them how much they are loved.

FOCUS

Final Thoughts

Let me clear about something: Fatherhood is not easy. My message is not meant to imply if you are present and connected in your children's lives that everything will always go smoothly. Life is, no doubt, a rollercoaster with many up and downs. But, I believe beyond a shadow of doubt that if we try to live by the five FOCUSed Father principles, our children will have a solid foundation for their lives ahead.

Of the thousands of words in this book, my hope is that the one you remember and take to heart is "Focus." That is the bottom line. As I've written, being a good dad isn't about doing all the right things, taking the best vacations, or saying all the right things. Being a good dad is about being active, involved, and present in your children's lives, which requires a clear focus on them.

I encourage you to make the *choice* to be a FOCUSed father, because it won't just happen. Life changes when we have children. Different decisions have to be made. You might not go to all the parties you did when it was just you and your spouse. You might not hunt or fish every opener or play every golf tournament as you did in the past. I ask you to make sure that *might* becomes *will*. If you *will* make the choices that put your children at the focal point, they *will* be given the best chance for a happy and productive life.

Our greatest responsibility as parents is to prepare our children for adulthood. We are preparing them to make good choices and lead productive lives. I was recently made aware of a great example of FOCUSed parenthood. Among the many fathers I spoke to as part of my research for this book, I spoke with a friend who is a local community leader. I feel he epitomizes the concept of my message. He and his wife have one son, who is sixteen years old as I write. For his fifteenth birthday he was given a car from his grandparents—a 1988 Oldsmobile with only 46,000 miles, and not one scratch. Because he wasn't sixteen, he couldn't use the car for a year. The plan was to store the car in the garage with a tarp covering it. Shortly after receiving the gift he told his parents he didn't want to keep the car. He said to his parents that it didn't feel right letting a perfectly good car sit in the garage unused, when the family already had two cars, and many people don't have any cars at all. He said he wanted to give the car to a Minneapolis-based charity that would give the car to someone who was in need. Wow! To say I am inspired by this story would be a gross understatement (especially as someone who loves cars). On his own, this young man decided to give away the car that was waiting for him. Values like caring for others and giving to others are not instilled without the involvement of FOCUSed parents.

Do you ever find yourself thinking about the good old days? Maybe it was high school. Maybe it was college. Those were times where we had little true responsibility, when we could do what we wanted when we wanted (within reason, of course). Over the past few years I have come to realize that I am actually living in the good old days *right now*. It's likely I will never do anything as important or fulfilling as providing a loving, nurturing upbringing for Emily and Kate. I suspect that when they are grown and have moved out, I will reflect upon these years fondly. I will miss the family dinners, and I will miss tucking them into bed every night. I will miss having them sitting in my lap. I will miss butterfly kisses and saying I love you many times a day. But, I believe that if I strive to be a FOCUSed father now, I will not look back and say "I wish I would have…" My hope and intention is that while I will miss having Emily and Kate with me every day, I will know I made the most of the time we had together, and that I, along with Beth, helped provide a foundation that ultimately allows them to be happy, productive adults. I also hope they will want to have the type of adult relationship with me as I have with my father.

Remember that your roles as husband and father are the two most important roles that you will ever have. In fact, our involvement in our children's lives is *crucial*. Don't take the responsibility lightly. Don't take the attitude that your wife will be the primary nurturer in your house. There is no mistake that children, boys and girls, benefit immeasurably from the involvement and guidance from fathers. When given the chance to choose how to spend your time, *choose* fatherhood. None of us will ever be perfect as fathers, but we can all strive for excellence in our effort.

Wherever you may be on your fatherhood journey, take one step forward. Maybe it's one more family meal a week. Maybe it's sticking to bedtime rituals. Maybe it's creating limits on screen time. Whatever it is for you, take one step forward. Be present, stay connected, be a FOCUSed father. God bless and happy fatherhood.

ABOUT THE AUTHOR

Chris Berg is a passionate father dedicated to helping dads see the power of their presence in their children's lives. He has been a featured speaker at parenting forums and conducted workshops aimed at giving fathers inspiration and tools to be present and connected with their children.

He is a board of directors member of Putting Family First (www.puttingfamilyfirst.org), an organization whose mission is to raise awareness about the crucial connections between parents and children and help families find balance in their lives.

Chris lives with his wife, Beth, and daughters, Emily and Kate, and Bear (the dog) in Medina, Minnesota. He can be reached at 612-655-0345 or chris@focusedfather.com.

ORDER FORM

1. Call 612.655.0345 and use your Visa, Mastercard or American Express or a company purchase order
2. Mail your order with pre-payment or company purchase order to:

   FOCUSED FATHER
   150 Prairie Creek Road
   Medina, MN 55340

3. Order Online at: www.focusedfather.com.

Product	Price	Quantity	Subtotal	TOTAL
The Focused Father	$11.95			
Shipping Costs: 1 book - $5.95, $.80 for each additional book. *Call for express rates*				
Order TOTAL				

Need more than one copy? We have quantity discounts available.

Quantity Discounts (Books Only)		
10–24 = *10% off*	25–99 = *25% off*	100 or more = *35% off*

Payment Methods: ☐ Credit Card ☐ Check ☐ Purchase Order PO# _____

Credit Card	Number	Expiration	AVS (3 digits)
Visa / Mastercard / American Express	– – –	/	
Cardholder address (if different from below):	Signature:		

Customer Information	
Name:	
Title:	
Company:	
Address:	
City, State, Zip:	
Daytime Phone:	
Email:	

Satisfaction guarantee: If you are not satisfied with your purchase, simply return the products within 30 days for a full refund.
visit www.focusedfather.com or call 612.655.0345.